Thanking Jesus

Nathan Moore

Published by Nathan Moore, 2023.

THANKING JESUS

First edition. September 11, 2023.

ISBN: 979-8223030232

Written by Nathan Moore.

Table of Contents

Thanking Jesus
By Nathan Moore

Acknowledgements

Scripture quoted by permission. All scripture quotations, unless otherwise indicated, are taken from the NET Bible® copyright ©1996-2016 by Biblical Studies Press, L.L.C. All rights reserved.

Preface

Groundwater can finally begin flowing through a pump at the surface of a well after water is added, priming the pump and initiating flow. Once the well is full from the additional water, groundwater can continue to be pumped out from the surface. This booklet aims to provide glimpses of Jesus: to prime the pump of intimate gratitude in response to Jesus for who He is, what He has done and what He promises to do — prompting a lifestyle flowing with thanking and obeying Jesus.

Each chapter is laid out in three sections: Meditate, Consider and Pray. Scriptures are in bold font. Read the Scriptures slowly. Most importantly, meditate on the implications of the Scripture's message. You may need to research each passage separately to understand its context. Read the considerations in the next section and respond to Jesus in heartfelt prayer and worship, as Mary Magdalene did after she saw Him newly resurrected. I can imagine Mary, years later, even when life became painful, remembering our resurrected Savior, and worshiping Him. These chapters were first written for me, as I synthesized who Jesus is and wanted to grow in responding to Him. I hope this booklet reminds you of our resurrected Savior and primes the pump of your heart to continue thanking Jesus.

-Nathan Moore

Introduction

The most important man of all time gave us far more than we realize. The glimpses of who He is and what He has done for us have resulted in centuries of heartfelt worship to Him in response. And just like He promised, temporary suffering has been common for those who have disregarded prestige, comfort and possessions — **compared to the far greater value of knowing Christ Jesus.**[1] The most published collection of writings in history unveil Him to be life's ultimate hero who triumphs over all evil.

"He is no fool who gives what he cannot keep to gain that which he cannot lose."[2] The most valuable things we can possess on earth now are worthless compared to Jesus. Why is He so valuable? Why does He deserve such allegiance and gratitude? Why is He more delightful than prestige and prosperity? God the Father delighted to send Jesus to us, who delighted entirely in His Father. Jesus knows the depths of our darkness and delights to redeem us into resurrected light, to finally be fully known and fully loved forever. Let's explore some glimpses of His gifts to us.

1 - An Opportunity

Meditate:

...an angel of the Lord appeared to him in a dream and said, "Joseph, son of David, do not be afraid to take Mary as your wife, because the child conceived in her is from the Holy Spirit. She will give birth to a son and you will name him Jesus, because he will save his people from their sins."[3]

Christ Jesus came into the world to save sinners.[4]

Consider:

We need to be saved from our sin. Sin is the beginning of destruction of goodness. Temptation can easily lead to sinful desire, where the destruction begins. Sin is a wrong and evil desire, or a word or deed against someone. It is an often invisible act of war prompting wrath in return. Forms of sinful desire include greed, hatred, idolatry, covetousness, slander, lust, arrogance, false accusations and laziness, among others. These desires war against God, others and ourselves simultaneously, while growing into intentions, words and actions.

The resulting shame can eat away at us, limiting relationships with everyone around us. But even when sin feels good, such feelings make it no less evil and destructive. Temporary feelings of pleasure, stress relief, power or significance resulting from sin lead to habit-forming addictions which foster destructive thought patterns. And just like healthy habits, destructive habits are contagious, becoming easily repeated. God has promised appropriate justice in a future judgment, in response to all sin.

The good news is that He sent Jesus to save us from our sins. We can belong to Jesus instead of being slaves to our sins. **God demonstrates his own love for us, in that while we were still sinners, Christ died for us.** [5] He desires intimacy with us while still justly punishing sin. He paid our debt so He can adopt us as His children.

Into the destructive drama of humankind entered Jesus, who never sinned but identified with our humanity. He represented us by receiving God's wrath in the place of anyone who trusts Him. He fulfilled ultimate love and ultimate justice simultaneously in His death. **In this is love: not that we have loved God, but that he loved us and sent his Son to be the atoning sacrifice for our sins.**[6]

He wants us to enter His kingdom: His lifestyle of thankfulness, love and obedience to God. Jesus is alive today in heaven. God the Holy Spirit now leads us on earth to enjoy a spiritual resurrection of sweet friendship with God, while we anticipate our resurrected life with Jesus in the future. Jesus gives us an opportunity for redemption.

Pray:

THANK YOU JESUS FOR offering Yourself to save me from my sins and for the opportunity to become adopted into Your loving and good family. Thank You for wanting to redeem me and transform me from my destructive thoughts and actions. Thank You for welcoming me into Your loving lifestyle of friendship with You. Thank You for being my Savior and my King. Thank You for being punished by God the Father instead of me. Thank You for being alive now and for sending me Your Holy Spirit to guide me. I trust You to no longer consider me an enemy of Yours, because You finished my just penalty for me on the cross. I trust You to give me eternal friendship with You. You have given me the privilege to be Yours, and I receive this opportunity. I am all Yours now! Thank You for purchasing me! Thank You for the opportunity to live a new life with You! Amen.

2 - Our Existence

Meditate:

He is the image of the invisible God, the firstborn over all creation, for all things in heaven and on earth were created in him – all things, whether visible or invisible, whether thrones or dominions, whether principalities or powers – all things were created through him and for him. He himself is before all things and all things are held together in him.[7]

All things were created by him, and apart from him not one thing was created that has been created.[8]

Consider:

Jesus participated with God the Father and God the Holy Spirit in lovingly designing and creating all things for His glory, and He continues to do so. We have a very limited knowledge of the vast work of creation and of Jesus' cooperation with His fellow persons in the Godhead. But we have enough understanding to respond by worshiping the all-powerful

Creator and Sustainer, Jesus. Jesus is the brilliant inventor, the engineer, the builder and the maintainer of everything. He sustains all the systems of the universe, both measurable and spiritual. He authored material architecture and brilliantly established the physical forces. Jesus continues to empower and limit the influence of everything and everyone.

He created each of us. He knows how many hairs are on our heads because all those hairs were made through Him and for Him. In fact, He made everything. Everything! Everyone! We are made to live creatively: living reminders of God Himself, crafted in His image.

His designs are more than material and mechanical. His moral design results in wonderful blessing upon perseverance in love and truth, yet destruction awaits arrogance and lies. He allows us to live in some of the painful consequences of sin, which helps us recognize our need for new life through His truth and love.

God the Father allows pain and suffering, to lead us to turn to Him. One stormy night, Jesus was out at sea with His panicked disciples as waves swamped the boat, threatening their lives. Then the Creator **got up and rebuked the winds and the sea, and it was dead calm. And the men were amazed and said, "What sort of person is this? Even the winds and the sea obey him!"**[9] He is trustworthy to provide redemption, even in seemingly hopeless circumstances. His power to save was demonstrated when His tragic crucifixion led to His resurrection. Human pain doesn't indicate God made an error. It shows we desperately need a Savior who can make all things new. It warns of the dire consequences of our rebellion against Him. Even in the most miserable circumstances, we are not Jesus' judge. He is our Judge. We fulfill our destiny when we love God and others from a thankful heart, knowing that we have already been loved. **For we are his creative work, having been created in Christ Jesus for good works that God prepared beforehand so we can do them.**[10] His intentions for us are redemptive, productive and good.

We desire a fully functional and loving environment. We long for much more than the ruined world around us, in desperate need of redemption. Our souls cry out for all things to be made new! While Jesus currently holds all things together for His glory, He has promised to make all things new in the future. He is the author, the judge and the restorer of His creation. When we trust Jesus for forgiveness, our spirits arise to new hope of complete future restoration. We experience this in part while we wait to see Him face to face. He will come again to earth, just as He left when He ascended to heaven. What a privilege to be reborn and belong to Him, to enjoy His love, justice and mercy!

Pray:

THANK YOU JESUS FOR creating all things in heaven and on earth, whether visible or invisible, whether thrones or dominions, whether principalities or powers. All things were created through You and for You. You have stretched out the heavens, and continue to do so. Thank You for Your design of humankind to bear Your image of love and to rule over Your creation. Thank You for fashioning me to live in Your kingdom of love, justice and mercy. Thank You for promising future justice, mercy and redemption of Your creation. Thank You for sealing Your promise with Your resurrection and giving us hope to be with You face to face — enjoying You and Your restored creation in the age to come. Amen.

3 - Our Identity

Meditate:

"But I will make a new covenant with the whole nation of Israel after I plant them back in the land," says the Lord. "I will put my law within them and write it on their hearts and minds. I will be their God and they will be my people. People will no longer need to teach their neighbors and relatives to know me. For all of them, from the least important to the most important, will know me," says the Lord. "For I will forgive their sin and will no longer call to mind the wrong they have done."[11]

While they were eating, Jesus took bread, and after giving thanks he broke it, gave it to his disciples, and said, "Take, eat, this is my body." And after taking the cup and giving thanks, he gave it to them, saying, "Drink from it, all of you, for this is my blood, the blood of the covenant, that is poured out for many for the forgiveness of sins.[12]

See what great love the Father has given us that we should be called God's children—and we are! The reason the world does not know us is that it didn't know him. Dear friends, we are God's children now, and what we will be has not yet been revealed. We know that when he appears, we will be like him because we will see him as he is. And everyone who has this hope in him purifies himself just as he is pure.[13]

Consider:

We can easily define ourselves by our jobs, our muscles, our politics, or our brains. Or perhaps by our sports teams, our wealth, our successes or our failures. God wants us to first be *His*. He is dead serious about purchasing us, having paid for our just punishment with the death of Jesus Christ. We don't have to let our sinful choices define us. If we trust Jesus, we have our primary identity in belonging to God, because He purchased us.

He knows us. He knows who we are now, and who He is creating us to be. He knows us more deeply than we know ourselves. He knows our inclinations, our actions, our hopes, and our loves. Through new birth by His Spirit we belong to Him as His children! He calls us to be the salt of the earth and the light of the world, by participating with Him in revealing Jesus' majesty. He wants us to enjoy the privilege of adoption into His royal family in the midst of people around us. Jesus invites us to call God our Father![14]

Our identity is attached to His identity. Jesus knows His own unique identity. He said, **"before Abraham came into existence, I am!"**[15] His unique human identity matches God's name which He revealed to Moses from a burning bush. After Jesus was baptized, just as He was coming up out of the water, the heavens opened and He saw the Spirit of God descending like a dove and coming to rest on Him. And a voice from heaven said, **"This is my one dear Son; in him I take great delight."**[16] Jesus started His ministry with assurance of knowing who He was, and that God the Father took great delight in Him. Jesus understands the power of a true identity. We must resist the temptation to believe lies that any identity is higher than belonging to Jesus. Politicians can tempt us to care most about belonging to a candidate or a party. We can lie to ourselves that our habits or ambitions define us. Belonging to our Savior outshines all other identities, even our family heritage.

Will you be a slave to temporary labels? Or will you belong to your loving Creator and Redeemer Jesus, who offered Himself as a sacrifice to save you? He lives today to delight in your participation with Him as part of His family. We are God's children if we trust Jesus to make us His royal family members. We get to celebrate our new identity — that we now belong to the almighty, all-loving, merciful Jesus. He is the ultimate treasure of all that exists. He established the New Covenant with anyone in humanity who is willing to be His bride. He writes

His law of love and mercy on our hearts. Our new identity is established by Him and centered on Him. In God's New Covenant in Christ, God defines us. **"I will be their God and they will be my people."**[17] The ultimate privilege in life is to belong to Jesus Christ!

Pray:

JESUS, THANK YOU FOR knowing my thoughts, my environment, my pain, my disappointment, my victories and my perspectives, from Your perspective. Only You have the ability to define me accurately. I can hide nothing from You, and I have a desperate need for You to forgive me for the sins I have committed. Thank You for sacrificing Yourself to make a New Covenant with me. Thank You for wanting me to belong to Your family of love and victory over death! Please save all the people around me as well! Thank You for redefining my life! I am not a slave to my reputation or my sins. You have purchased me! Thank You for making me yours! Thank You for the highest privilege in life, to be Your child! Thank You, Holy Spirit, for showing me my need for salvation and making me a new creation in Christ! Thank You, Father, for loving me by sending Jesus so I would not perish but have eternal life! I trust You, Jesus, with my whole life, to be my Redeemer now and forever! Thank You for the amazing privilege of being Yours! You are amazing! You are my King, and You are enough for me! Help me to reject all sin and temptation to desire anything more than You. You are my treasure, my King and my best friend. Thank You for Your defining covenant of love! Amen.

4 - His Example

Meditate:

Each of you should be concerned not only about your own interests, but about the interests of others as well. You should have the same attitude toward one another that Christ Jesus had,
who though he existed in the form of God
did not regard equality with God
as something to be grasped,
but emptied himself
by taking on the form of a slave,
by looking like other men,
and by sharing in human nature.[18]

"and whoever wants to be first among you must be your slave - just as the Son of Man did not come to be served but to serve, and to give his life as a ransom for many."[19]

"If I then, your Lord and Teacher, have washed your feet, you too ought to wash one another's feet. For I have given you an example - you should do just as I have done for you."[20]

Consider:

Jesus became one of us. He is a real human being who felt the pain and suffering we all feel. He was tempted in all the relentless ways we are tempted. He understands us completely and empathizes with our experiences.

He is the supreme example of submission to God throughout an earthly painful life, surrounded by sin and temptation. He left His divine environment and made Himself of no reputation. While on earth, He lived in persistent submission to God the Father while being situationally aware of His physical, spiritual and social environment. He loved God more deeply than we realize, because He knew that God was His loving Father. He loved people because He knew His true Father loved people. He denied Himself the pleasure of giving into sinful temptation because His true Father is too amazing to be replaced by pleasure. He did not envy the popularity and prestige of the religious leaders of His time because He possessed the far greater treasure of God the Father's approval.

Although He had no sin to repent of, He joined repentant sinners when He was baptized, only to hear the audible voice of the Father declaring great pleasure and initiating His public ministry. He desired the glory of God more than His own reputation when He forcefully challenged the high-class, religious salespeople of His time to seek God in prayer when in the temple, instead of seeking personal fortune.[21] He trusted God even while looking foolish to others during His trial. He loved the outcasts and was ridiculed as one of them; then celebrated God's resurrection power with them.

Jesus gave everything, every bit of energy and affection to God. He is our true example. He said **"I have come down from heaven not to do my own will but the will of the one who sent me."**[22] The kingdom of God was demonstrated in Jesus' earthly life because God the Father was the only King He served.

Pray:

OH GOD, WE ARE NOT worthy of Your adoption because we have loved other things, including ourselves, more than You. Thank You, Jesus, for Your earthly example of loving God the Father with Your entire being, resisting sin, and becoming a ransom for me by taking my punishment on the cross. Thank You for loving God more than Your reputation. Thank You for having mercy on the outcasts, including me, and for promising me resurrected life in Your kingdom forever. Help me to live in the kingdom of God now by loving God with all my strength, because You have first loved me. Thank You for the perspective You maintained on earth: the supreme value of God and the value of people. Help me to follow Your example of love. Jesus, You are my King! You are my Redeemer! You are my example! Help me to serve others because You first served me. Amen.

5 - His Commitment To Us

Meditate:

This saying is trustworthy:
If we died with him, we will also live with him.
If we endure, we will also reign with him.
If we deny him, he will also deny us.
If we are unfaithful, he remains faithful, since he cannot
deny himself.[23]

"My sheep listen to my voice, and I know them, and they follow me. I give them eternal life, and they will never perish; no one will snatch them from my hand. My Father, who has given them to me, is greater than all, and no one can snatch them from my Father's hand."[24]

Consider:

Jesus is committed to us, like the best husband is committed to His bride. If we cheat on Him, He remains our faithful and best lover. Those of us who trust Jesus to save us have entered into a lifelong and eternal covenant with Him.

He delights in shaping us toward perfection, and somehow wants us to be His spiritually intimate lover. Jesus wants us to be His eternal companions and co-laborers in His mission to expand the Kingdom of God.

When a man proposes to marry the woman he loves, he wants an equally passionate commitment in response. After loving us with all His heart, God wants us to love Him with all our hearts. When we don't love Him with all that we are, our sin remains destructive in the full sight of God, who knows our every thought. He desires honest confession, acknowledging reality and turning back to Christ in thankful repentance. He also cares about the people we have hurt in the process and wants us to reconcile with them. When faced with the options to hide our past sin, justify our past sin, or confess our past sin to those affected, confession is our only beneficial choice.

A faithful lifestyle from the heart builds trust in any relationship, leading to productive teamwork. Yet who among us hasn't broken God's trust? Thank God that Jesus' payment on the cross is greater than our sins against Him, whether from the past, present or the future.

His call to repentance is not simply to turn from sin to a determination to abstain from sin. Repentance is turning from sin *to Jesus,* who knows us and invites us to reside with Him in a future without death, mourning, crying or pain. Our bad habits will eventually be part of the former things that have ceased to exist. We, who depend on His simultaneous justice and mercy on the cross, receive Jesus' eternal commitment of loving redemption. He leads us in our dance to return to Him, turn after turn, all the while pledging His faithfulness to us. We remain His, as we dance with Him throughout our lives, while we wait to see His face.

Jesus is committed to the best version of us. He is fully loving, holy, productive and humble. We all too often don't feel like living a loving, holy, productive and humble life. Yet Jesus offers us a cross-shaped engagement ring. His mercy and resurrection strength gently lead us to lay down our pride and marvel at the beauty of His love. He joyfully welcomes us into His family of humble love for each other. The one who commanded the sea to be still commands us to be holy, to respond to God with complete love, and resist destructive temptations to love anything else more than Him.

He has not saved us into a system of belief or simply into heaven's reservation list. We are engaged to Jesus Christ who is our judge, faithful rescuer and eternal king. If anyone can make an eternal commitment of redemption, renewal and eternal friendship, it is our eternal Savior Jesus Christ, the most powerful lover in all existence.

Pray:

THANK YOU JESUS THAT if I am unfaithful, You remain faithful to me because You cannot deny Yourself. You are my kind Savior. Your commitment surpasses any human promise possible because it is pure, utterly loving, and truly happily ever after. Your commitment is stronger than death and never ending. Thank You for loving me with eternal reasons to delight in You. Though I have sinned against You, You have given me eternal life. I am delighted to be fully known and fully yours for eternity! Thank You for walking through life with me now, and lovingly leading me forever. I love You too. Amen.

6 - His Leadership

Meditate:

"Come to me, all you who are weary and burdened, and I will give you rest. Take my yoke on you and learn from me, because I am gentle and humble in heart, and you will find rest for your souls. For my yoke is easy to bear, and my load is not hard to carry."[25]

"I give you a new commandment – to love one another. Just as I have loved you, you also are to love one another.[26]

Then Jesus came up and said to them, "All authority in heaven and on earth has been given to me. Therefore go and make disciples of all nations, baptizing them in the name of the Father and the Son and the Holy Spirit, teaching them to obey everything I have commanded you. And remember, I am with you always, to the end of the age."[27]

Consider:

Jesus is the best king possible. He knows us thoroughly and loves us faithfully and eternally. He leads us in the most satisfying purpose imaginable, to multiply heartfelt love for God and others! Our lifestyle of love for God and people is led by Jesus' lifestyle of love for God and us. He calls us to enjoy God, and in turn to desire the best and to do good for others, to the fullest extent we can.

The pain we experience as we follow Jesus is both temporary and worthwhile as we imitate our Savior, who, for the joy set before Him, endured the cross. In the same way, we also have joy set before us. Our great king is our treasure, worth loving with all our strength and all our possessions. Our great companion is our leader, who is with us in every situation. He knows the cost of true love, and provides future hope and present strength for us to love Him and others in every way He leads us to.

Jesus gives us the privilege of participating in His work: to expand His kingdom to more parts of our lives, and to the lives around us which we affect. We get to participate in the greatest kingdom in existence right now. Our thoughts, ambitions, relationships, and actions can beautifully express love for our Father God and others, because He first loved us. The kingdom of God is living God's ways because of His love expressed through Jesus. He leads our motivations to respond to our mighty God, living with awareness of our kind God who loves us and others, including our enemies. Jesus rose from the dead to lead us forever. Forty days after His resurrection, He clarified that all authority had been given to Him. He instructed us to live out His commands, knowing that He is always with us. What a friend we have in Jesus! He leads us to enjoy and live out true love.

Pray:

THANK YOU, JESUS, FOR leading me and teaching me to live in Your kingdom of love for God and love for others, because of Your love for me. I desire Your glory now and forever! I desire goodness and mercy for the people around me, even those who hate me. I forgive those who have wronged me, and ask for Your help to never seek revenge, but instead to love because You love me. Thank You for leading my thoughts, words and actions to be for Your glory and the good of people around me. Thank You for the privilege of participating in Your kingdom. Please lead my heart back to You whenever I am tempted to sin. You are my best friend, and I love you! Amen.

7 - His Correction

Meditate:

"When the Son of Man comes in his glory and all the angels with him, then he will sit on his glorious throne. All the nations will be assembled before him, and he will separate people one from another like a shepherd separates the sheep from the goats. He will put the sheep on his right and the goats on his left."[28]

The good person brings good things out of his good treasury, and the evil person brings evil things out of his evil treasury. I tell you that on the day of judgment, people will give an account for every worthless word they speak. For by your words you will be justified, and by your words you will be condemned."[29]

My child, do not despise discipline from the Lord, and do not loathe his rebuke. For the Lord disciplines those he loves, just as a father disciplines the son in whom he delights.[30]

Consider:

God's good warning of fair, future, final justice is part of His correction to us today. We desire appropriate justice but we don't know enough details of circumstances or intentions to know what good justice would even look like. Jesus is the judge who promises supreme justice, with a reckoning for all thoughts, words and actions in the future, final judgment. God's anger is an expression of His love because holiness is loving the good, and rejects all evil. Yet He nailed our sins to Jesus' Cross and loves to mercifully invite us to Himself. **The Lord is not slow concerning his promise, as some regard slowness, but is being patient toward you, because he does not wish for any to perish but for all to come to repentance.**[31]

While He expects us to administer fair, temporary interpersonal justice on earth as well as we can, Jesus will be the ultimate moral judge. All our sins are against God, even when they are directed toward other people because He loves those people - and any evil on earth is an offense to His creation. One day, Jesus will punish all people with just, fierce, eternal punishment in hell, unless they have become part of His kingdom by relying on His payment on the cross. His corrective warning now is actually part of His mercy leading us to salvation.

We must distinguish between judgment and correction. Jesus' judgment resulting in eternal punishment of evil will not be undone. Do not wait to turn to Jesus. His *correction* today is part of His mercy to us now, inviting us to join Him in His redemptive kingdom of love for God and others. We cannot outsmart God by living for ourselves and hoping God's promise of punishment wasn't serious. No one is more sincere than Jesus, the embodiment of all goodness and love. He eternally opposes all rebellion against love.

God's anger is not opposed to His love. It is an expression of it. Jesus the judge died for our sins and rose from the dead to bring us into His merciful kingdom. We need Jesus because He is the only one who has paid for our sins, which are ultimately against Him.

Jesus provides us at least two types of corrections in this life. The first is His warning to turn from evil to delight in His passionate mercy that rescues us from our sins and future judgment. The second is His ongoing training to grow in loving God and loving people because He loves us and purchased us. When a religious expert asked Jesus which commandment in the law was the greatest, **Jesus said to him, "'Love the Lord your God with all your heart, with all your soul, and with all your mind.' This is the first and greatest commandment. The second is like it: 'Love your neighbor as yourself.' All the law and the prophets depend on these two commandments."**[32]

It can be tempting to resist God's correction because of past hurts or lingering questions. It can be tempting to be bitter toward God for difficult circumstances. But God does not answer to us. We will answer to Him, who understands our circumstances better than we do. We are the clay, and He is the potter. We are created, and He is the Creator. Our understanding is limited; His is limitless. We must appreciate what He has shown us while acknowledging the mysteries that He has not shown us. He has not revealed *why* life can seem so unfair, but He has given us the opportunity to turn to Him for rescue and participate in His redemption. While He welcomes our honest questions, they are no reason to resist God's correction. We must humbly trust Him to lead us through correction, persecution and other suffering in life, trusting that He causes all things to **work together for good for those who love God, who are called according to his purpose.**[33] Ultimately, we need Jesus Himself rather than answers to any objections to Him. Even when it is humbling, it is a privilege to be corrected by Jesus now because He is drawing us to a deeper friendship with Him.

We know that God is in earnest because **he has set a day on which he is going to judge the world in righteousness, by a man whom he designated, having provided proof to everyone by raising him from the dead**[34]. Jesus' earliest followers, who ate, walked and talked with Him in resurrected form, went on to suffer ridicule, imprisonment and execution by those who opposed Jesus and His message of repentance and forgiveness. These early followers would not have endured such pain unless they truly saw the resurrected King, being convinced of His power, truth and love. It was for the joy set before them, in a present worship and hope of future resurrection, that they thanked Him with a sacrifice of their earthly, temporary comfort, to love Him and others instead.

Jesus is worthy of our entire lives, and those who were closest to Him on earth knew His immeasurable value. John, one of His closest followers, referred to Jesus as the Word of God, writing: **"Now the Word became flesh and took up residence among us. We saw his glory – the glory of the one and only, full of grace and truth, who came from the Father."**[35]

Correction is intended to help us when it comes from those who love us. Such correction can be very painful, yet far better than our naturally destructive ways. His corrections can also be wonderfully freeing. If He corrects sin in your thought life, you may endure painful changes in how you live. You may be embarrassed or suffer physical pain. He prunes those He loves. He wants our affections to be for Him, not for our reputation or for old ways. His correction is a gift to us for His loving kingdom, for our good and the good of those around us.

Pray:

THANK YOU, JESUS, FOR warning us of Your future just punishment of sin. Thank You for being honest with us about Your coming judgment. Thank You for offering us good, life-saving correction! I turn to you, Jesus, and thank You for being holy, without sin, and full of truth and love. Thank You that You do not passively tolerate evil. Thank You for being fully against all kinds of evil, for correcting me, paying for my sin by Your death on the cross. Jesus, please save those around me from Your judgment and help them listen to Your correction; to trust You for forgiveness, instead of trusting themselves. Thank You for considering me and those around me to be valuable enough to die for. Thank You for desiring a good future for me, despite my sin. Thank You for acting on my behalf. Help me to imitate Your love! Help me to love You and love the people around me. Help me to recognize Your astounding value as well as the value of those around me. Help me to act according to Your desires and for the good of those around me. Thank You for being my kind Savior! Help me enjoy You in every circumstance, even the painful ones, as I anticipate future resurrection with you! Amen.

8 - His Complete Sacrifice

Meditate:

When he had received the sour wine, Jesus said, "It is completed!" Then he bowed his head and gave up his spirit.[36]

By his will we have been made holy through the offering of the body of Jesus Christ once for all.[37]

For by one offering he has perfected for all time those who are made holy.[38]

The Son is the radiance of his glory and the representation of his essence, and he sustains all things by his powerful word, and so when he had accomplished cleansing for sins, he sat down at the right hand of the Majesty on high.[39]

Consider:

We do not need to wonder if God exhaustively punished our sins through Jesus' crucifixion. Our punishment was completed! "**...the Lord caused the sin of all of us to attack him.**"[40] Are you included in all of us? Then your sin attacked Jesus. The eternal God-Man was a sacrificial substitution for the eternal punishment we deserve. All people are redeemable. *Whoever* relies on Jesus becomes adopted into His family. Whoever does not rely on Jesus remains outside His kingdom, because living in His kingdom includes reliance on Him. No more sacrifices are needed in order to enjoy adoption by God.

Jesus represented us. He was the only perfect human representative capable of bearing the full justice of God for all of humankind when He died on the cross. He is **the Lamb of God who takes away the sin of the world!**[41] The metaphor of the lamb of God reminds us of when God saved the enslaved Israelites from God's wrath on Egypt. During the tenth plague on Egypt, known as the Passover, God's angel of death killed the firstborn sons in all the Egyptian households, but passed over and spared those who had the sacrificial blood of a lamb painted on their doorposts. The Passover feast was subsequently celebrated annually, including a lamb's sacrifice by a priest, as a reminder to the Israelites of God's merciful salvation from slavery. Over one thousand years later, Jesus was killed during the annual Passover festival, ironically at the command of Israel's jealous high priest. He was actually God's final sacrifice for sin. The cross was painted with Jesus' blood. Those of us who rely on Him are free from God's future judgment against sin. We are on a journey with His leadership — for the remainder of our earthly lives and beyond. Our journey's next destination will be coming face to face with Jesus in the promised spiritual heaven and then the future physical resurrection in the renewed heavens and earth.

The detailed nature of God's future judgment remains mysterious to us. We do not know each other's hearts, but God does. His judgment will be fair and merciful from His holy and righteous perspective. He desires everyone to turn to Him in gratitude instead of remaining in sinful self-reliance. Sufficient payment was made for anyone to trust Jesus' complete payment of their past, present and future sins. **If you confess with your mouth that Jesus is Lord and believe in your heart that God raised him from the dead, you will be saved.** [42] Your gratitude for adoption into Jesus' good and loving family is one evidence that you have received Him to be your king and have entered His kingdom. Jesus' sacrifice is complete. While on the cross, **when he had received the sour wine, Jesus said, "It is completed!" Then he bowed his head and gave up his spirit.** [43] We celebrate victory with Him by rejoicing in His complete sacrifice and resurrection triumph over death, now and forevermore!

Pray:

THANK YOU JESUS FOR completing Your sacrifice for me! I need You and am overwhelmed by Your loving desire for me to live in Your kingdom with You — now and forever. I delight in Your love for me. All my sins have been paid for by Your death! All my past, present and future sins are forgiven! Thank You for considering me now as if I am only loving. Thank You for kindly changing me, and for promising to completely restore my body to be purely devoted to You in the future as well. I delight in You now because Your redemption includes living in Your kingdom of gratitude and love — for You and others — while I wait to be fully transformed in my body. I am thrilled to grow in love with You for the rest of my life. And I look forward to the full resurrection of all that I am, to enjoy You in eternal loving harmony. You have given yourself as a loving sacrifice and You are my most faithful lover. I take You to be my king and my best friend, both now and forever. Thank You Jesus for Your faithful, eternal love for me. Amen.

9 - His Intercession For Us

Meditate:

... he holds his priesthood permanently since he lives forever. So he is able to save completely those who come to God through him, because he always lives to intercede for them. For it is indeed fitting for us to have such a high priest: holy, innocent, undefiled, separate from sinners, and exalted above the heavens.[44]

"Worthy is the lamb who was killed
to receive power and wealth
and wisdom and might

and honor and glory and praise!"[45]

Consider:

Thomas the disciple needed to see Jesus's pierced hands and side in order to believe that Jesus was alive. Even in Jesus' resurrected body, He kept His scars as a statement in that He completed the ultimate payment for sin.

Jesus is now in heaven at the right hand of God the Father, with the same scars in His hands and side. Jesus continues advocating for his people, displaying a constant reminder of His submission to God to the Father and His love for His people. Jesus remains continuously committed to the Father and to us. All the creatures in heaven recognize Him as *the* lamb who was killed and lives to be worthy of all worship.

We can feel condemned when we remember our own sins. **But God, being rich in mercy, because of his great love with which he loved us, even though we were dead in transgressions, made us alive together with Christ—by grace you are saved! —and he raised us up with him and seated us with him in the heavenly realms in Christ Jesus, to demonstrate in the coming ages the surpassing wealth of his grace in kindness toward us in Christ Jesus. For by grace you are saved through faith, and this is not from yourselves, it is the gift of God;**[46]

Jesus was our intercessor on the cross before we were born; and He has been our intercessor during our life's journey as well. Before we trusted Him, we were spiritually dead. But once we trusted Him, we were restored to be born again into His family. He *wants us* to be His people. It is not that He loves us because we are valuable. Without His intercession, we are destructive rebels worth punishing. Yet, we have been given restored value because He loves us and adopted us to be in His family. Today in heaven, Jesus collaborates with God the Father and God the Holy Spirit to restore us to enjoy Him and His loving lifestyle.

As our good shepherd, Jesus leads us today to live with confidence in His continuous mercy; and to forgive those who sin against us. He leads us to a life of being loved, and of loving; of being healed and of offering healing; of being lavished and of living generously. He leads us away from worry and fear by reminding us of His reliable promises of full redemption. He still works on our behalf by interceding for us, and He will not let anyone condemn us. **Who is the one who will condemn? Christ is the one who died (and more than that, he was raised), who is at the right hand of God, and who also is interceding for us.**[47]

Pray:

THANK YOU JESUS FOR interceding for me. Thank You for dying and rising from the dead to bring me into Your kingdom! Thank You for collaborating with God the Father on my behalf. Thank You for wearing in Your nail-scarred hands the proof that You paid for my sins. You are my lover and leader. Thank You for Your constant work to love the Father and to love me. You are worthy to receive power and wealth and wisdom and might and honor and glory and praise! You are more than the sacrificed lamb because You are also the resurrected lamb! Thank You for seeing every offensive detail of my sin-saturated soul and choosing to intercede for me to be Your forgiven, loved, and clean family member. You are my healer, restorer and advocate. I come to God by relying on You to be my eternal intercessor, leader and best friend. Thank You Jesus. Amen.

10 - Heaven

Meditate:

"Do not let your hearts be distressed. You believe in God; believe also in me. There are many dwelling places in my Father's house. Otherwise, I would have told you, because I am going away to make ready a place for you. And if I go and make ready a place for you, I will come again and take you to be with me, so that where I am you may be too. And you know the way where I am going."
Thomas said, "Lord, we don't know where you are going. How can we know the way?" Jesus replied, "I am the way, and the truth, and the life. No one comes to the Father except through me.[48]

Then I saw a new heaven and a new earth, for the first heaven and earth had ceased to exist, and the sea existed no more. And I saw the holy city - the new Jerusalem - descending out of heaven from God, made ready like a bride adorned for her husband. And I heard a loud voice from the throne saying: "Look! The residence of God is among human beings. He will live among them, and they will be his people, and God himself will be with them. He will wipe away every tear from their eyes, and death will not exist any more - or mourning, or crying, or pain, for the former things have ceased to exist."[49]

Consider:

Jesus became one of us on earth in a physical body, suffering temporarily with an eternal perspective. **For the joy set out for him he endured the cross, disregarding its shame, and has taken his seat at the right hand of the throne of God. Think of him who endured such opposition against himself by sinners, so that you may not grow weary in your souls and give up.**[50] While on earth, Jesus anticipated returning to closer fellowship with God the Father at the right hand of His throne. He also looked forward to creating new heavens and a new earth, to live with us there forever in our resurrected bodies! He was the first to enjoy the new life He promised, when He rose from the dead in a physical, immortal body. He rejoiced in the opportunity to express loving redemption to rebellious people, to save those of us who would have Him as our king.

What will it be like to live eternally in the new earth? Consider the breathtaking details Jesus put into creating the existing earth and universe. Even more so, God will celebrate His victory by inaugurating a detailed, creative environment, allowing us to live out more amazing eternal lives than we can imagine. He is our creative God! We will finally be at rest with

God! We will finally be at peace with each other! We will work productively. Life will finally work! We will live without fear. We will be continuously assured of God's powerful love. We will finally love God and one another as we desire to — with all our hearts. We will experience the most engaging life possible.

Jesus has a spiritual heaven presently waiting for those who die before He returns. He is also preparing a renewed earth where we will experience our full potential for living with God. We can anticipate having excellent working memories, deep joy celebrating Jesus, and productive fresh purposes and responsibilities. He will lead us without the limitations of sickness and aging. Laughter and love will be our new normal. He is building a place with no more tears, pain, or sorrow. Our Savior will rescue us from our sins, regrets, pain and death. He will bring us into His presence forever because He loves us. And He will be there.

Pray:

THANK YOU JESUS FOR wanting to live with me in Your kingdom forever! You have good thoughts toward me, and I am so privileged to belong to You. Thank You for thinking through the details of creating the new heavens and the new earth as our future home. Thank You for the opportunity to look forward to the future with joyful anticipation in the midst of suffering on earth. May Your kingdom come on earth as it is in heaven, where You are loved completely because You are worthy, righteous, holy and completely loving. Amen.

11 - Promising Us The Holy Spirit

Meditate:

"If you love me, you will obey my commandments. Then I will ask the Father, and he will give you another Advocate to be with you forever - the Spirit of truth, whom the world cannot accept, because it does not see him or know him. But you know him, because he resides with you and will be in you."[51]

"I have spoken these things while staying with you. But the Advocate, the Holy Spirit, whom the Father will send in my name, will teach you everything, and will cause you to remember everything I said to you."[52]

So Jesus said to them again, "Peace be with you. Just as the Father has sent me, I also send you." And after he said this, he breathed on them and said, "Receive the Holy Spirit."[53]

But the fruit of the Spirit is love, joy, peace, patience, kindness, goodness, faithfulness, gentleness, and self-control. Against such things there is no law.[54]

Consider:

One marvelous evidence of Jesus' role as God the Son was His ascension to heaven. The Father answered Jesus' prayer to return to His side and be glorified with the glory that Jesus had with the Father before the world was created.[55] His disciples realized that His ascension marked the beginning of His royal intercession for them from heaven. They then joyfully waited for the Holy Spirit to give them power to be His witnesses, thanking and obeying Him in all kinds of circumstances and places. The disciples knew that even their physical deaths in the future could not separate them from the love of God. They had seen their resurrected king ascend into heaven. That ascension proved His promise: **"I am the resurrection and the life. The one who believes in me will live even if he dies, and the one who lives and believes in me will never die."**[56] They were delighted to be part of His kingdom! And now we have this same privilege! If we believe in Jesus, even if we die, we have His promise of amazing life with Him forever! Jesus has promised to return, just as He ascended. If we die before His return, our spirits will join Him in heaven, awaiting physical resurrection for eternal life in the new heavens and new earth.

Right now we have the privilege of glorifying God on the earth which He created. Humanity's rebellion and the world's resulting brokenness can't stop us from honoring Him here and now. We are often tempted to sin against God in a variety of ways. Numerous lies routinely assault our ears and minds. Jesus knows the spiritual battle is real, which is why He sent the Spirit of truth to be with us. God is a good Father who gives His Holy Spirit to those who ask.[57] The Holy Spirit strengthens us to respond to God and the world around us with confidence in His victory — the victory that comes through Jesus' death, resurrection and ascension. The Spirit teaches us the **good news about Jesus the Messiah, the Son of God**[58] and reminds us of Jesus' teachings. He helps us partner with Jesus in life, love God with all our strength, care for others as we care for ourselves, and savor the privilege of this lifestyle.

Jesus was physically God with us on earth. Yet He is now at the right hand of the Father in heaven. He said, **"it is to your advantage that I am going away. For if I do not go away, the Advocate will not come to you, but if I go, I will send him to you. And when he comes, he will prove the world wrong concerning sin and righteousness and judgment - concerning sin, because they do not believe in me; concerning righteousness, because I am going to the Father and you will see me no longer; and concerning judgment, because the ruler of this world has been condemned.**

"I have many more things to say to you, but you cannot bear them now. But when he, the Spirit of truth, comes, he will guide you into all truth. For he will not speak on his own authority, but will speak whatever he hears, and will tell you what is to come. He will glorify me, because he will receive from me what is mine and will tell it to you. Everything that the Father has is mine; that is why I said the Spirit will receive from me what is mine and will tell it to you. In a little while you will see me no longer; again after a little while, you will see me." [59]

Jesus is part of the one and only Triune God, who is like no one and nothing else in all existence. We have the privilege of living in the kingdom of God the Father, God the Son and God the Holy Spirit. Jesus, God with us, has ensured that God remains with us always, to the very end of this age.[60] God has graciously chosen for us to be led by His Holy Spirit, guiding us through life on earth while Jesus intercedes for us on His royal throne in Heaven. The Spirit reveals God to us, glorifies Jesus, and energizes us to live fruitful lives. God loves us joyfully, peacefully, patiently, kindly, faithfully, gently and intentionally. He leads us to love others in the very same ways.

Pray:

THANK YOU HOLY SPIRIT for guiding me! Thank You Jesus for being my King in heaven, advocating for me. Thank You Father for having mercy on me by sending the King of all things as a sacrifice, to bear the punishment for my sins against you! You are worthy of more love than I could ever give. I delight to be safe in Your arms. Death will not have the final word on me. I trust

You Jesus to take me by Your nail-scarred hands and welcome me into heaven, to rejoice in Your eternal salvation! Thank You Holy Spirit for the privilege of understanding Your truth. Thank You for inspiring me to live a life of love, joy, peace, patience, kindness, goodness, faithfulness and self-control. Thank You for comforting me, strengthening me, and encouraging me to love You and love others, as You remind me of the love of Jesus. Amen.

12 - Revealing God The Father

Meditate:

John testified about him and shouted out, "This one was the one about whom I said, 'He who comes after me is greater than I am, because he existed before me.'" For we have all received from his fullness one gracious gift after another. For the law was given through Moses, but grace and truth came about through Jesus Christ. No one has ever seen God. The only one, himself God, who is in closest fellowship with the Father, has made God known.[61]

Now a certain man, a Pharisee named Nicodemus, who was a member of the Jewish ruling council, came to Jesus at night and said to him, "Rabbi, we know that you are a teacher who has come from God. For no one could perform the miraculous signs that you do unless God is with him." Jesus replied, "I tell you the solemn truth, unless a person is born from above, he cannot see the kingdom of God."[62]

Consider:

All humanity wants to see God, yet God the Father is a Spirit who has not allowed us to see Him directly. God told Moses, **"You cannot see my face, for no one can see me and live."**[63] When Philip, one of Jesus' disciples, recognized Jesus' unique relationship with God the Father, He said, **"Lord, show us the Father, and we will be content." Jesus replied, "Have I been with you for so long, and you have not known me, Philip? The person who has seen me has seen the Father! How can you say, 'Show us the Father'? Do you not believe that I am in the Father, and the Father is in me?**[64]

Jesus, God the Son, revealed God the Father to the people around Him during His earthly ministry. He lived as the fully human expression of God, taught people about God, and personally demonstrated God's love and power. The Father spoke audibly to validate Jesus' sonship and authority — both at Jesus' baptism and His transfiguration. Jesus taught people authoritatively about the kingdom of God and performed loving miracles throughout Judea and Samaria. His Sermon on the Mount prepared people to see their need for God's salvation, and He subsequently revealed himself as the Savior. **For God did not send his Son into the world to condemn the world, but that the world should be saved through him.**[65] When crowds asked Him, **"What must we do to accomplish the deeds God requires?" Jesus replied, "This is the deed God requires - to believe in the one whom he sent."**[66]

His teaching about the nature of God included parables, using word pictures with spiritual truths that often offended proud hearers. Yet those same parables drew humble hearers to fresh devotion toward God. For example, in the parable of the two sons, the father lovingly celebrates the humble return of his rebellious son, while his prideful son refuses to join the celebration. Proud people resist God and humble people recognize their need for Him. Similarly, **"God opposes the proud, but he gives grace to the humble."**[67]

Jesus said that God is a spirit. He revealed the character of God the Father to be good, just, faithful, authoritative, powerful, perfect, patient and merciful. God the Father sees our thoughts, loves us, desires our love toward Him in response, and wants us to reflect His mercy toward others. Jesus revealed that God is more valuable than anything or anyone on earth, and yet He hears our prayers and can be trusted because He cares about us. As we relate with the Holy Spirit, with Jesus, and with the Father in thankfulness and obedience, our revelation of God and our relationship with Him will grow for all eternity.

Pray:

THANK YOU, JESUS, FOR revealing God the Father to us. Thank You that He is our loving Father. Thank You for revealing His amazing life-restoring power which resurrected You from the dead. Thank You for coming to earth, becoming human, and loving us, welcoming us into Your kingdom. Thank You for revealing that God the Father is worth obeying, even in the most painful circumstances. Please lead my thoughts and perspective of You as I grow in love with you. You died to demonstrate Your love for us, and You are alive, loving us even now. Your power is the greatest in all existence. You have promised to re-create the heavens and the earth. You love me with an everlasting love, and have removed my sin as far as the east is from the west. You have promised that the pure in heart will see God, and I thank You for letting me see You indirectly now. I long to see you, and God the Father, face to face in heaven, just as You promised. Amen.

13 - Thanking Jesus

Meditate:

Now on the way to Jerusalem, Jesus was passing along between Samaria and Galilee. As he was entering a village, ten men with leprosy met him. They stood at a distance, raised their voices and said, "Jesus, Master, have mercy on us." When he saw them he said, "Go and show yourselves to the priests." And as they went along, they were cleansed. Then one of them, when he saw he was healed, turned back, praising God with a loud voice. He fell with his face to the ground at Jesus' feet and thanked him. (Now he was a Samaritan.) Then Jesus said, "Were not ten cleansed? Where are the other nine? Was no one found to turn back and give praise to God except this foreigner?" Then he said to the man, "Get up and go your way. Your faith has made you well."[68]

Consider:

Imagine that you promised an enemy of yours a lifesaving present and showed him the receipt of your purchase. How would you know if your enemy was willing to receive the gift? Gratitude would evidence that your enemy believed that you were capable of providing that gift, and was counting on you to obtain it. Jesus' resurrection is the receipt that His death purchased our complete redemption. It proves His intent to resurrect us, without moral punishment, into renewed life with Him as our King. **For the payoff of sin is death, but the gift of God is eternal life in Christ Jesus our Lord.**[69]

Jesus Christ came to earth to seek and save the lost.[70] **For this is the way God loved the world: He gave his one and only Son, so that everyone who believes in him will not perish but have eternal life.**[71]

Jesus compared the people around Him to sheep without a shepherd. Adam and Eve were deceitfully tempted to distrust God. So they rejected God's rule by eating the forbidden fruit of the tree of knowledge of good and evil. They preferred the knowledge of good and evil over trusting God's direction. They believed the lie that their envisioned god-like status was more valuable than the leadership of God Himself. Because of their rejection of God, God drove Adam and Eve out of the Garden of Eden. This banishment cut them off from the tree of life, resulting in inevitable death and the end of their amazing communion with Him. We have a rebellious heritage based on lies that God is not good enough. Now, we too are like sheep without a shepherd.

Humanity does not inherently live in loving communion with God. We are not automatically in harmony with the world around us, and we often struggle to enjoy harmony with one other. Throughout our history, human rebellion has revealed itself in evil, selfish and destructive ways. Our good God will punish all evil thoughts, words and actions in a final, fair judgment.

But God loves us and wants to have mercy on us. God revealed Himself in Jesus' human body to show us His mercy. He lived perfectly in loving obedience to God the Father while suffering and resisting temptation. Jesus was punished on our behalf when He died on the cross, finishing God's punishment of all our evil. He was restored to life bodily within three days and now lives in eternally loving communion with God the Father in heaven.

Jesus is the human expression of God and king of the universe. He also is the one who will judge us all by His standard of righteousness. Yet, redemption is now available to us!

His gift is free: Himself as our king. His kingdom means living in passionate, thankful, loving communion with God and restored relationships with others. Do you believe Jesus can provide this gift to you? Are you counting on Him to obtain this gift?

Worship Him! Thank Him with all your strength! He offers us loving freedom from His wrath and a restored lifestyle as sheep enjoying and trusting the good shepherd. We are not merely saved into the location of heaven. We are saved into Jesus' leadership, into restored loving communion with God, into a thankful lifestyle of enjoying Him and His ways. Jesus wants more than just to forgive us; He wants us to respond in joyful relationship with Him.

We are not victims, but beneficiaries of His mercy. So, let's not waste our lives complaining about our circumstances. Jesus is alive and loves us! He has given us an opportunity to enter His kingdom! He has given us our existence, our identity, His example, and His commitment to us. He has given His leadership, His correction, His complete sacrifice, and His constant intercession for us. We have heaven to look forward to, the Holy Spirit as our companion now, and the manifestation of God Himself! Thank You Jesus!

Pray:

THANK YOU JESUS FOR overwhelming me with Your love. You promised eternal life in the restored community of Your loving family. You have extended Your pierced hands to rescue me from the misery of sinful living and from Your fierce, thorough justice. Thank You for being far greater than I realize, and far stronger than all my sin. Thank You for thinking about me and the people around me. Thank You for wanting us to belong to you. Thank You for Your correction, and for Your good intentions toward me. Who else can I turn to but you? You alone are the king of all kings and the embodiment of true love. You are worth more than all I am and all I have. I am Your child and You are my Savior, leader and friend! Thank You Jesus!

---

[1] Philippians 3:8b

[2] *The Life of the Rev. Philip Henry, A.M.* p. 35 (1839) by Matthew Henry. Also, 1949 Journal Excerpt from Jim Elliott (*Shadow of the Almighty* (1989) by Elisabeth Elliot).

[3] Matthew 1:20b-21

[4] 1 Timothy 1:15

[5] Romans 5:8

[6] 1 John 4:10

[7] Colossians 1:15-17

[8] John 1:3

[9] Matthew 8:27

[10] Ephesians 2:10

[11] Jeremiah 31:33-34

[12] Matthew 26:26-28

[13] 1 John 3:1-3

[14] See Matthew 6:9

[15] John 8:58b

[16] Matthew 3:17b

[17] Jeremiah 31:33b

[18] Philippians 2:4-7

[19] Matthew 20:27-28

[20] John 13:14-15

[21] See Matthew 21:12-14

[22] John 6:38

[23] 2 Timothy 2:11-13

[24] John 10:27-29

[25] Matthew 11:28-30

[26] John 13:34

[27] Matthew 28:18-20

[28] Matthew 25:31-33

[29] Matthew 12:35-37

[30] Proverbs 3:11-12

[31] 1 Peter 3:9

[32] Matthew 22:37-40

[33] Romans 8:28

[34] Acts 17:31

[35] John 1:14

[36] John 19:30. Jesus' statement while dying on the cross.

[37] Hebrews 10:10

[38] Hebrews 10:14

[39] Hebrews 1:3

[40] Isaiah 53:6

[41] John 1:29b

[42] Romans 10:9

[43] John 19:30

[44] Hebrews 7:23-26

[45] Revelation 5:12b

[46] Ephesians 2:4-8

[47] Romans 8:34

[48] John 14:1-6

[49] Revelation 21:1-4

[50] Hebrews 12:2-3

[51] John 14:15-18

[52] John 14:25-26

[53] John 20:21-22

[54] Galatians 5:22-23

[55] See John 17:5

[56] John 11:25

[57] See Luke 11:13

[58] Mark 1:1

[59] John 16:7-16

[60] See Matthew 28:20

[61] John 1:15-18

[62] John 3:4

[63] Exodus 33:20b

[64] John 14:8-10a

[65] John 3:17

[66] John 6:28-29

[67] James 4:6b

[68] Luke 17:11-19

[69] Romans 6:23

[70] See Luke 19:10

[71] John 3:16

Don't miss out!

Visit the website below and you can sign up to receive emails whenever Nathan Moore publishes a new book. There's no charge and no obligation.

https://books2read.com/r/B-A-TMKAB-RNWNC

BOOKS 2 READ

Connecting independent readers to independent writers.

About the Author

Nathan Moore is growing in love with Jesus, who purchased him on the cross. He gets to live with his fabulous wife Emily and 4 fantastic children, currently in Baltimore, Maryland.